Reflections on the Stations of the Cross
by Terence J Brain
Emeritus Bishop of Salford

alive Publishing

First published in 2019 by Alive Publishing Ltd
Graphic House, 124 City Road, Stoke on Trent, ST4 2PH
Tel: +44 (0) 1782 745600 • Fax: +44 (0) 1782 745500
www.alivepublishing.co.uk • email: booksales@alivepublishing.co.uk

© 2019 Alive Publishing. British Library Catalogue-in-Publication Data. A catalogue record for this book is available from the British Library.

All rights reserved. No part of this publication may be reproduced or transmitted in any form or by any means, electronic or mechanical, including photocopying, recording or any information storage and retrieval system, without either prior permission in writing from the publisher or a licence permitting restricted copying.

In the United Kingdom such licences are issued by the Publishers Licencing Society Ltd, 90 Tottenham Court Road, London W1P 9HE.

Imprimatur: Archbishop Bernard Longley, 2019.
Nihil Obstat: Fr Paul Dean MA, STB, MA. The nihil obstat and imprimatur are official declarations that a book or pamphlet is free from doctrinal or moral error. No implication is contained therein that those who have granted the nihil obstat or imprimatur agree with the content, opinions or statements expressed.

ISBN: 978-1-906278-35-9

Cover image: Norman Adams RA
© St Mary's (The Hidden Gem), Mulberry Street, Manchester, M2 6LN

Contents

Introduction 7

First Station: Jesus is condemned to death - Ecce Homo................................... 14

Second Station: Jesus receives the Cross 22

Third Station: Jesus falls the first time under His Cross 28

Fourth Station: Jesus meets His Blessed Mother 32

Fifth Station: The Cross is laid upon Simon of Cyrene 40

Sixth Station: Veronica wipes the face of Jesus 44

Seventh Station: Jesus falls the second time 48

Contents

Eighth Station: The women of
Jerusalem mourn for our Lord 52

Ninth Station: Jesus
falls the third time 56

Tenth Station: Jesus is
stripped of his garments 60

Eleventh Station: Jesus
is nailed to the Cross 64

Twelfth Station: Jesus
dies on the Cross 68

Thirteenth Station: Jesus is
taken down from the Cross
and placed in the arms of
His Blessed Mother 72

Fourteenth Station: Jesus
is buried in the tomb 76

Introduction

Who hasn't, at times, gone into a church with the primary intention of not praying but of looking? For example, St Peter's in Rome, St Paul's in London, St Mark's in Venice are full of 'visitors', some of whom may say a prayer, but all will look: admire the architecture, the paintings, the statuary, et cetera. They say beauty is in the eye of the beholder but each beholder may not be moved by the same beauty. You often hear people saying things like: 'What's it meant to be?', or 'Lovely, beautiful; I could sit here all day just looking.' People will find beauty in small buildings as well as large; simple styles as well as ornate; strong colours as well as gentle colours. It is a personal response but a personal response that is formed by our experience and culture.

The different styles of architecture from Romanesque through Perpendicular to

Modernism and everything in between; the different schools of art that are represented in paintings; the different forms of statues and crucifixes: even the church plate and vessels are very different according to the period in which they were designed and made.

In 1994 Canon Denis Clinch, the then parish priest of St Mary's Mulberry Street in Manchester – also known as The Hidden Gem – commissioned from the artist Norman Adams RA a set of Stations of the Cross. These were solemnly erected in the church in 1995 in the presence of the Duchess of Kent.

As works of art the Stations were well received: they had been exhibited at the Royal Academy prior to being delivered to the Hidden Gem. Norman Adams believed them to be his finest work, and he has written how in preparing to paint these works he felt the need to experience a real closeness to Christ – a one to one relationship with him. I came to Salford as

Bishop in 1997, and I visited the Hidden Gem informally to see the new Stations.

St Mary's Mulberry Street, as we have it today, is a small Victorian church. The dimensions and the decoration of the church are in balance and represent the style of their day. The new Stations of the Cross contrast sharply with the style of the rest of the church. I was struck by the power of the whole set of the paintings and also felt that they were, in a sense, constrained by the space available to hang them. When I mentioned to people that I had visited the Hidden Gem and thought that the new Stations of the Cross were very powerful, I was surprised by the number of people who responded by saying that they didn't like them.

I had found them strong and challenging, commanding me to look at them. Not quite 'in your face' but certainly not quiet and demure. Here was raw emotion, but much more than just raw emotion. Here were paintings that told a story in paint and form; told a story that I knew well. But here, it was told in a language I was not used to hearing. Or more strictly seeing, I was not used to seeing this style of painting to depict the story of the Passion, and that explained to me why people didn't like them. They were not able to see a story they knew well because they were not used to seeing it in the way Norman Adams had depicted it. Since it was different they did not see what they expected to see. So they did not like what they actually saw.

This little book is an attempt to help people to understand the language that is paint and form in these beautiful stations. If we cannot begin to 'read' the paintings, we will not find the story: and that means we will not come into the church to use the Stations to pray. And that defeats the purpose of having them.

Stations of the Cross are in churches to tell the story of the events that we know as the redemptive act of Christ – his passion and death on the cross, leading to his resurrection and ascension into heaven. The telling of this story moves us to contemplate the subject of the story, Jesus Christ, and to respond in prayer: Here I am, Lord, I come to do your will as you came, in response to the Father's will, to deliver us from all evil.

I have more to say about some of the Stations than I have about others. Sometimes it is because I want to show you the symbolism of colour and shape in religious art. Sometimes it is because I can see several strands of thought for prayer in the same picture.

The following pages are my interpretation of the Norman Adams stations: others may interpret them differently. My purpose is to help you 'read' the pictures: let them speak to you so that you can speak to God.

I have not offered a formal set of prayers other than to end each Reflection with the prayer: 'I love you Jesus, my love, above all things', and a verse of the hymn *Stabat Mater Dolorosa*, uniting ourselves with Our Lady and how she pondered in faith the mystery of our redemption. Whether you read this booklet at home or in front of the Stations in the Hidden Gem, I wanted to leave you with a 'composition of place', a place you can enter and spend some time with the One you love, because he first loved you.

God so loved the world that he sent his son born of a woman; a man like us in all things but sin.

First Station
Jesus is condemned to death – Ecce Homo

Many people go and stand in a bookshop and read the first chapter of a book to see if it appeals to them before they buy it. Either that or they buy the book because they liked the cover. A lot of time and effort goes into the design of book covers because, so often, they are the first thing that draws us into buying a book. When we stand in front of Norman Adams' 'Stations of the Cross' we are standing in front of a story: not in a book but hanging on the wall in pictures. The Stations of the Cross is the story, the true story that recounts the last hours of Christ's redeeming life. Like any well told story it will begin by introducing us to the main character.

This first Station is the book cover, the first chapter, the thing that captures our attention and our desire to 'read' this story. The first Station introduces us to Jesus: who he is, why he is here and what he is doing. Time spent here, looking at the first Station will help us to enter into the whole story so that we come to know Christ.

<u>So, behold the man – Ecce homo.</u>

Behold the man, Jesus, the suffering servant foretold by the prophet Isaiah. It is with the words of Isaiah in our ears that we look up at the painting. 'Like a sapling he grew up in front of us, like a root in arid ground. Without beauty, without majesty, no looks to attract our eyes' (Is 53:2). Certainly there is little here to attract us! We cannot recognise here the personal image we have of Christ. Perhaps that is because so often our image of Christ is just that – a personal image - and not an image true to the Christ who spoke of himself as 'one with the Father'. Our understanding of Christ can so often be no more than an imagination: this is how I want Christ to look and be. So perhaps we need to ask the question St Paul asked Christ on the road to Damascus: Who are you Lord?

St Paul must have often thought about that moment, when Christ came into his life and changed it forever. In his second letter to the church in Corinth he reminded them: 'Recognise the grace of our Lord Jesus Christ; although he was rich he became poor for our sake, so that through his poverty you might become rich.' (2 Cor 8:9) Here, we see Christ in that poverty. Here, we see the Second Person of the Trinity, Christ, who came into the world to redeem us on a cross. God made man, stripping himself of his majesty and riches and revealing the suffering servant of the Lord God.

Looking at this first Station we see Christ stripped down to his raw humanity: stripped down to his very DNA. Again looking at this Station we see a cross that is part of the face of the Lord. It almost grows out of his face! Adams has stripped the face of Christ down to its raw DNA, and his double helix is the Cross. Seeing this we realise that the Cross is Christ's purpose; his *raison d'etre*. This is the reality of who Christ is. Christ, the Son of God, who in the gospels reminded his disciples the he had come not to do his own will but to do the will of his Father; and he and the Father are as one in this purpose. And this will, this purpose, culminates in the raw suffering of the passion and death of Christ on a cross. This is an awful thought, one we are not comfortable with: it is no wonder that this first Station shocks us.

This is the man whom Pontius Pilate presented. This is the man questioned by Pilate: 'Are you a king?' This is the man who replied to his question: 'Yes. I am a king. I was born for this. I came into the world for this: to witness to the truth: and all who are on the side of truth listen to my voice' (John 18:37). Pilate could not see the king standing before him and presented Christ 'Behold the man'. At first glance we too cannot see the king, we barely see the man. Yet when we look more carefully we can see the Eternal Son, Christ the King.

Eyes are described as 'the windows of the soul' and when we look at the eyes of Christ in this first Station we see that Adams has painted them red and blue. The colour red symbolises the human nature of Christ and the colour blue symbolises the eternal divine nature of Christ: Two natures, one person. The person of Christ is staring out at us, suffering for love of us, asking us: 'My people, what have I done to you? How have I offended you? Answer me' (Reproaches: Good Friday Liturgy).

Here, we see Christ made sin; remember the words from Scripture that Jesus was man in all things but sin. Now we see him 'made sin'. That is also why this picture disturbs us. The sinless one has become sin in order to redeem us from that sin which is ours not his. Yet all the ugliness of sin cannot hide the beauty of God's eternal love. And as we look upon this face dominated by the cross we move up from the awful red terror of the agony in the garden, up through the scourging and crowning with thorns, up following the cross through the rays of green hope, up, out of the picture into the realm of God, the Eternal Father. Those that have eyes to see, see!

And all the time those eyes of Christ, the beloved Son - the flower of the Father - are telling us: Yes: I am the way, the truth, the life. Follow me, trust me, accept me, receive me.

'Thus in the cross and him who hung upon it, all things meet, all things subserve it, all things need it. It is their centre and their interpretation' (Bl John Henry Newman).

I love you Jesus, my love above all things. I repent with my whole heart of having offended thee. Never permit me to separate myself from thee again, and grant that I may love thee always and then do with me what thy wilt.

At the cross her station keeping,
stood the mournful mother weeping,
close to Jesus to the last.

To be a follower of mine, take up the Cross and follow me.

Second Station
Jesus receives the Cross

Let us look and contemplate.

Put aside what you expect to see when looking at the Second Station because this picture in front of us is not like the normal depictions of Jesus receiving his Cross. What do we see?

The first thing to catch our eye is the bright golden cross: it dominates, draws us into the picture and draws us to itself. This Cross is precious. This Cross is the instrument of redemption for all who handle it; and we see two hands on the Cross. The one hand, holding the weight of the Cross, belongs to the person giving the cross to Christ. The other hand, reaching up, is that of Christ receiving the Cross.

After noticing the Cross we become aware of the two heads, one red one black. The red head is the person giving the Cross to Christ, and Christ is at the bottom of the picture depicted in the dark hues. We can see the crown of thorns around his head. So the whole picture is created with three main colours: red, gold, and black.

In the symbolic language of religious art, these colours are used to speak of humanity and human nature (red); the eternal and divine is seen in the colour gold. And the colour black, in this context, denotes death and the grave.

Now we can look and see the story in this Station.

Are we looking at an individual giving the Cross to Christ; or are we seeing the whole of humanity, all of us, giving the Cross to Christ? This red figure is almost hiding behind the Cross as if subconsciously acknowledging that what is being done is not just.

We see that the golden Cross is dividing the top half of the picture from the bottom half of the picture : and also, on the top to bottom axis, the Cross connects the two heads together. The cross is a cross road for us to navigate. St Mark (8:34) recalls Christ's words to his disciples: 'If anyone wants to be a follower of mine, let him renounce himself and take up his cross and follow me.'

Earlier in the same chapter Mark recalls Christ asking the disciples who they think he is. Simon Peter spoke up: 'You are the Christ'. Can we see Christ the Son of God here, or is it a dead man walking? The dark sombre colouring of Christ certainly points to a dead man, but when we look more closely we see in his painted hand the outline in red, and around the crown of his head we see hints of gold. Human and Divine: two natures, one Person: The Christ, the Son of God: The Way, the Truth and the Life.

So now we look and see what we didn't see to begin with. We see a role reversal. The giver is now the receiver, and the receiver is now the one who is giving; giving his life for our redemption.

I love you Jesus, my love above all things. I repent with my whole heart of having offended thee. Never permit me to separate myself from thee again, and grant that I may love thee always and then do with me what thy wilt.

Through her heart, his sorrow sharing,
all his bitter anguish bearing,
now at length the sword had passed.

My eyes are worn out with suffering

Third Station
Jesus falls the first time under His Cross

Christ is tumbling head over heels. This painting is dark, disturbing, yet it is not a painting of despair. The darkness is lightened with blue, red and gold. Blue is the dominant colour in the flowers around the edges of the painting and in the eyes of Christ in the top half of the painting. As in the First Station the eyes are painted in blue and red - the two natures of Jesus Christ, the beloved Son who is one with the Father Creator of heaven and earth.

Looking at the painting we see Christ falling head over heels: by the painting of the mouth in the top image of Christ we can see the alarm as he realises that he is falling. In the lower images we see the disorientation and, perhaps, even concussion looking at the round red eye of the second image of Christ's head: you can feel the 'bang' as he hits the ground. And the momentary blacking out of concussion is reflected in the painting of the eye in the third head image. This first fall was violent, and it hurt.

Yet all around the painting are the gold highlights reminding us that the Father is with him giving him the strength to fulfil his mission: the yolk will become easier, the burden lighter.

You have deprived me of my friends,
made me repulsive to them,
imprisoned, with no escape;
my eyes are worn out with suffering.
I call on you, Lord God, all day,
I stretch out my hands to you. (Ps 88:8-9)

Truly, O God, I am your servant:
I am your servant, the son of your handmaid;
you have released my bonds. (Ps 116:16)

I love you Jesus, my love above all things. I repent with my whole heart of having offended thee. Never permit me to separate myself from thee again, and grant that I may love thee always and then do with me what thy wilt.

Oh how sad and sore distressed
was that mother highly blessed,
of the sole-begotten One!

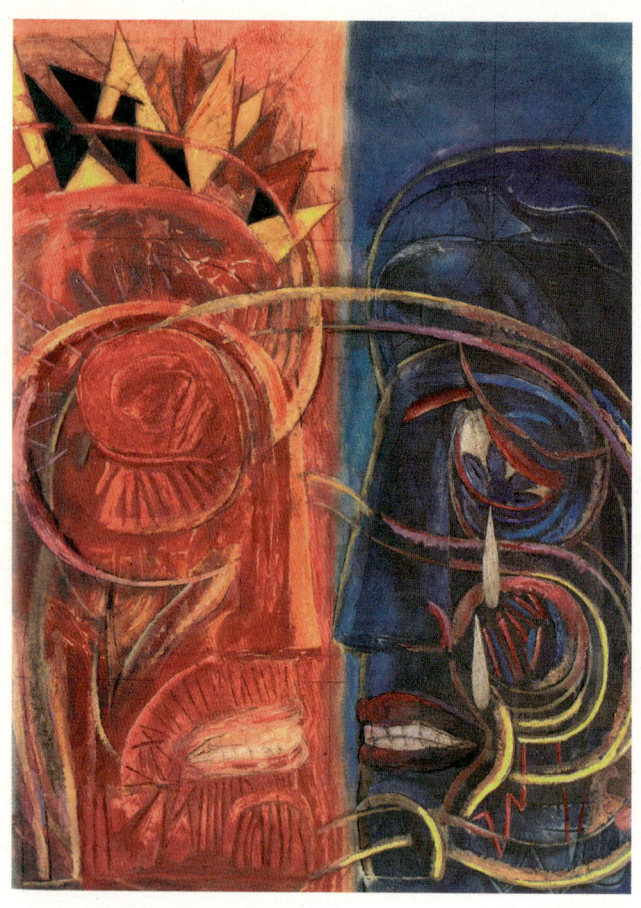

Anyone who does the will of my Father in heaven is my brother and sister and mother.

Fourth Station
Jesus meets his blessed mother

Here is a painting of two halves; one of Christ (red) and the other of Our Lady, his mother (blue). Let us begin with the Christ, the red half, and spend a moment or two looking and contemplating.

We see Christ still feeling the effects of his fall (his eye is closed), but the face of Christ, even with the bruised eye, is not the face of a broken man but a noble face. It reminds me of the Christ that is depicted on the earliest crucifixes: In pain and suffering from his trials, yes, but not defeated. This is the Christ who heard the voice of the Father when he was baptised in the River Jordan: 'This is my beloved Son in whom I am well pleased'. This is the same Christ who was transfigured on the mountain in front of the disciples Peter, James and John and again the voice of the Father was heard to declare 'This is my beloved Son – listen to him'.

The disciples would recognise these words as coming from the prophet Isaiah: 'Here is my servant whom I uphold, my chosen one' (42:1); and again in Isaiah 'You are my servant through whom I shall manifest my glory' (49:3).

This is not a futile life coming to its end (Isaiah 49:4). While there is the red of pain and suffering there is also, particularly in the crown of thorns, the golden colour and the lozenge shape. Gold is the colour that implies the eternal and the diamond or lozenge shape implies the divine, the Godhead. Here the colour and shape is telling us, through Christian symbolism, that this man is the Christ, the beloved of the Father, the one we have to listen to.

'All the while my cause was with the Lord God and my reward with my God. And now the Lord God has spoken, who formed me in the womb to be his servant, to bring Jacob back to him and to re-unite Israel to him; - I shall be honoured in the Lord God's eyes, and my God has been my strength' (Isaiah 49:4-5).

This is the Christ 'formed in the womb to be his servant': this is the Christ that we saw revealed in the First Station whose life is never futile but always with the purpose to reflect the Father's will 'so that my salvation may reach the remotest parts of the earth' (Isaiah 49:6b).

This is the same Christ whom Peter, when asked by him at Caesarea Philippi 'who do you say I am?' replied: 'You are the Christ the Son of God'.

Can we make the same affirmation of faith?

Now, let us turn to Our Lady, depicted in blue. Blue is the colour of heaven and Our Lady is, we believe, the only person who is presently both body and soul in heaven, enjoying the full benefits of her Son's redemptive life and death. So for this reason the tradition in religious paintings developed of depicting her as dressed in blue. So we greet her 'Hail Mary full of grace: the Lord is with thee: blessed art thou among women and blessed is the fruit of your womb, Jesus' (Luke 1:28ff).

The big tears running down Our Lady's face catch our attention. They remind us of the sadness of this moment, meeting her son on his way to crucifixion. The tears also take us back to the beginning of Christ's life when, as a baby, he was brought to the Temple and Simeon saw him as 'the Light of the World': Simeon also prophesied that his mother's heart would be pierced by the sword of suffering (Luke 2:33). An intensity of suffering brought about by the intimate bond between this mother and her child. This mother, full of grace, has always shared in Christ's life and mission – even now.

Look into her eye: Norman Adams tells us he painted it as a crescent moon, reflecting the light of the Son – the light of the world. 'God made the two great lights: the greater light to govern the day, the smaller light to govern the night... God saw that it was good' (Genesis 1:16). How often do we experience Our Lady in our lives as the kindly light amid the encircling gloom leading us onwards to her son?

Our Lady's eye is clear and bright contrasting with the bruised eye of Jesus. Is it clear and bright because we see the beginning of the next tear welling up? Or is it clear and bright because Our Lady is 'full of grace' and even now her faith burns brightly. Even in such tragic conditions she still trusts in the Lord God: 'My soul magnifies the Lord, and my spirit rejoices in God my Saviour' (Luke 1:45). 'Holy is his name: his mercy is from age to age to those who fear him' (Luke1:49).

Even now as she looks at her son, her child, God's gift to her, the fruit of her womb, she knows that he is also God's gift to the whole world: His beloved Son; her beloved son and now, our beloved Son.

And as we step back and look at the painting as a whole we can see the circling, twisting cord of gold and red-purple binding mother and son together, a symbolic umbilical cord. The mother gave the son human life: the Son gives his mother and us a share in the life of the Father.

I love you Jesus, my love above all things. I repent with my whole heart of having offended thee. Never permit me to separate myself from thee again, and grant that I may love thee always and then do with me what thy wilt.

Christ above in torment hangs;
she beneath beholds the pangs
of her dying glorious Son.

Shoulder my yoke and learn from me

Fifth Station
The Cross is laid upon Simon of Cyrene

A friend in time of need is a friend indeed: particularly when the friend was not looking to be a friend, but the act of friendship was imposed on him by others. Simon of Cyrene, we are told in the Gospels, was made to carry the cross.

In the Fifth Station we have Simon, painted in pink, reaching over to take hold of the cross from Christ who is painted below in sombre colours. Pink reflects compassion and hope: the hope that he, Christ, will now be strong enough to fulfil his mission. The compassion that enters Simon changes what began as a compulsory task into a privilege and a joy to help this man in need: a need that is all consuming, drawing the strength and life out of him; the dark night of the soul.

We can see Simon's strong hand lifting the weight of the cross from Christ on to himself. As we saw in the Second Station, Norman Adams has used the cross as a device to divide the two on the horizontal plane and also joining the two on the vertical, suggesting that the relationship between them is more than at first appears. The Cross of Christ is at the centre bonding both together. It is at our centre too: there to help us make our way to the Father – especially when we are faced with a decision we don't wish to face.

'Come to me all you who labour and are overburdened and I will give you rest. Shoulder my yoke and learn from me, for I am gentle and humble in heart, and you will find rest for your souls. Yes, my yolk is easy and my burden light' (Matt 11:28ff).

I love you Jesus, my love above all things. I repent with my whole heart of having offended thee. Never permit me to separate myself from thee again, and grant that I may love thee always and then do with me what thy wilt.

Is there one who would not weep,
whelmed in miseries so deep
Christ's dear Mother to behold?

Here I am Lord, come to do your will

Sixth Station
Veronica wipes the face of Jesus

The story of Veronica wiping the face of Our Lord is not found in any of the Gospel accounts of the Passion, so how it became one of the Stations of the Cross is a bit of a mystery. There are several legends that are in part an explanation but the truth is shrouded in history as is the human motivation that formed the legends. Whatever the origin was of the Veronica story, it is now a fixture in the Stations of the Cross and as such can be used to deepen our prayer when we meditate on the Stations.

One of the things that I am conscious of when praying the Stations of the Cross is the role played by women. We meet women four times in the Stations. In the Fourth Station we meet Mary; in the Sixth we meet Veronica; in the Eighth we meet the Women of Jerusalem and in the Thirteenth we meet Mary again as *Pietà*.

The Stations with the women in reflect loving compassion and gentleness towards Jesus, contrasting with the violence and anger shown towards him in the other Stations. Norman Adams has captured this sensitivity with the colours he uses in the sixth, eight and thirteenth Stations.

Looking at Veronica, the dominant colour is the golden yellow. First in the gentle face of Veronica, which then leads us down to her hands and arms cradling the cloth that bears the image of Christ. There is a gentleness and sadness here: petal-like tears run from her eyes.

With her long hair, untidy across her face and laced between her fingers, this painting reminds me of the event in the Gospel where a woman washed Christ's feet with her tears and dried them with her hair: another act of loving compassion (Lk 7:38).

Look at the image of Christ on the cloth. This is painted in a naive style – it could almost be a cross-stitch pattern that Veronica had made sitting by the fireside at home on winter evenings. There is something very personal here. And maybe that is what the legend in the Sixth Station is inviting us to contemplate: the individual personal bond that is present between Christ and each one of us. After all we believe that we are made in his image and likeness. How do I portray him? Can others see Christ in me? Am I a true icon (a veronica) of Jesus the Lord?

I love you Jesus, my love above all things. I repent with my whole heart of having offended thee. Never permit me to separate myself from thee again, and grant that I may love thee always and then do with me what thy wilt.

> Can the human heart refrain
> from partaking in her pain,
> in that Mother's pain untold?

Father glorify your name

Seventh Station
Jesus falls the second time

When we look at this Station, in the top half we see the raw red colour of pain and suffering: and the red colour appears to be leaching out, just as the strength and life of Christ is leaching out in this second fall.

In contrast, the lower half of the painting is worked in strong colours particularly in the reds, blues, yellows, gold and whites of the crown of thorns that, to my mind, symbolise here the Divine. And looking at the lower face of Christ in this painting, it is painted in two distinct colours almost as two different persons, or a person part in light and part in shadow. There is more here than just the vivid pain and suffering of a physical fall. The dark night of the soul that we felt in the Fifth Station is here too, but the black is pushed into the background by the colours of the crown of thorns.

This Second Fall draws us into a meditation on the person of Jesus Christ. It points to his human frailty being supported, lifted up and sustained by Divine strength: it reminds us of the unity there is between the Father and the Son: 'I am in the Father and the Father is in me' (Jn 14:10). This Second Fall paints a progression from that dark night of doubt into the light of conviction: Father, glorify your name.

'Now my soul is troubled.
What shall I say:
Father, save me from this hour?
But it is for this very reason
that I have come to this hour.
Father, glorify your name!
A voice came from heaven, "I have glorified it, and I will again glorify it".' (Jn 12:27-8)

I love you Jesus, my love above all things. I repent with my whole heart of having offended thee. Never permit me to separate myself from thee again, and grant that I may love thee always and then do with me what thy wilt.

For the sins of His own nation
saw Him hang in desolation,
all with bloody scourges rent.

My beloved Son: listen to him

Eighth Station
The women of Jerusalem mourn for our Lord

By now, we are used to looking at Adams' paintings and understanding his way of telling the story of the procession to Calvary through his large faces – a device to bring us into an intimacy with the characters, particularly with Christ: and we are used to seeing the flower-eyes as a symbol of the tenderness of the Lord's love for his Father and for us. And now this Eighth Station reminds us of the power of love.

The love of mothers for their children; the love expressed in the compassion of the women for the Lord; the love of the Lord for his Father; and the root of all this love, the love of the Father for His Son and all His Creation.

Looking at this Station I was drawn to the conversation of Jesus with Nicodemus in John

3:16ff. 'As Moses lifted up the snake in the desert, so must the Son of Man be lifted up so that everyone who believes may have eternal life in him. For this is how God loved the world: he gave his only Son, so that everyone who believes in him may not perish but have eternal life.' When Jesus says to the women 'do not cry for me' he is affirming that what he is doing, walking to Calvary, is what he came into the world to do. And it was love that caused him to come into the world: and it is love that drives him now on this last journey. And it all makes sense to him and is worth the cost, because this love is coming to him from the Father.

Look back to the First Station and recall the words of Jesus recorded in St John's Gospel 'Have I been with you all this time and you still do not know me: to have seen me is to have seen the Father.' What did the women of Jerusalem see when they grieved for him?

Could they understand that his journey was worth the cost? I hope so, because as mothers they have the experience of maternal love and will have experienced the fact that this love had a cost for them as mothers: but the cost doesn't stop them loving their children.

Love overcomes all.
Where you find love, you will find God.
Ubi caritas et amor, Deus ibi est!

I love you Jesus, my love above all things. I repent with my whole heart of having offended thee. Never permit me to separate myself from thee again, and grant that I may love thee always and then do with me what thy wilt.

Bruised, derided, cursed, defiled,
she beheld her tender child,
till His Spirit forth he sent.

Do not be afraid

Ninth Station
Jesus falls the third time

The first thing to catch your eye in this last fall is the bright golden splash of colour in the top half of the painting followed by the strong colours in the crown of thorns. This is the golden colour from the Eighth Station leading us on into the next painting.

This colouring is in stark contrast to the darkness of the first fall and the raw suffering in the second fall. But as we have progressed along the way, Christ has taught us to see him as he is. 'Who do people say I am? Who do you say I am? You are the Christ, the Son of the living God' (Matt 16: 13ff). 'This is my beloved Son in whom I am well pleased' (Matt 3:17). We should be able to make these words our own now, and if our faith is strong enough then we can say with Blessed John Henry Newman:

'Lead kindly light amid the encircling gloom, lead thou me on;
the night is dark, and I am far from home, lead thou me on.
Keep thou my feet, I do not ask to see the distant scene: one step enough for me.'

The encircling gloom is in this picture but it doesn't matter because the loving radiance of God is stronger than the darkness of the night of fear. Christ is not afraid at this fall: Christ is not overwhelmed by the pain of this fall. Fear and pain don't matter.

'So long thy power hath blest me, sure it still will lead me on,
o'er moor and fen, o'er crag and torrent, till the night is gone....'
(*Lead Kindly Light*, Blessed John Henry Newman)

I love you Jesus, my love above all things. I repent with my whole heart of having offended thee. Never permit me to separate myself from thee again, and grant that I may love thee always and then do with me what thy wilt.

O, thou Mother, fount of love,
touch my spirit from above,
make my heart with thine accord.

Thy will be done on earth as it is in heaven

Tenth Station
Jesus is stripped of his garments

In 595 AD, Pope St Gregory the Great, sent St Augustine on a missionary journey to England. You will remember he was the Pope who saw the Angle slaves in Rome. Seeing beyond their slavery he saw the image of God in them, and said: 'These are angels not Angles'. Pope Gregory also wrote commentaries on the Scriptures, and in particular for our purposes is a Commentary on the Book of Job.

Sometimes the character Job speaks as a person who sees a good life as sufficient to merit God's blessings – 'I am doing the best I can so God will bless me.' Sometimes the character of Job speaks as the Lord and shows that God's purpose is deeper and other than what we expect and presume. It is this idea that we now meditate on, looking at this picture.

In the picture we see the figure of Christ's face, his hands on either side of his cheeks. It reminds me, at first sight, of the painting known as *The Scream* by Edvard Munch, a painting that is associated with feelings such as despair, hopelessness. But this painting by Adams more alludes to the Book of Job rather than to Munch.

'My face is red with tears, and shadow dark as death covers my eyelids. Nonetheless, my hands are free of violence, and my prayer is pure. Cover not my blood, O earth...I have a witness in heaven, my defender is there on high' (Job 16:16ff).

This is not a man afraid, who feels deserted by God. This is a man who trusts that even in all this perceived agony and failure, God knows what he is doing. I can trust him.

Strip the clothes off; reveal the true Christ and we will see that he and the Father are one in mind and will. They have a higher purpose, and the shouting, screaming voices seen here surrounding Christ cannot defeat him, because he is surrounded even more closely by the love of the Father.

I love you Jesus, my love above all things. I repent with my whole heart of having offended thee. Never permit me to separate myself from thee again, and grant that I may love thee always and then do with me what thy wilt.

Make me feel as thou has felt;
make my soul to glow and melt
with the love of Christ our Lord.

*Behold the Lamb of God,
who takes away the sin of the world*

Eleventh Station
Jesus is nailed to the Cross

This Station has similarities to the Second Station, Jesus receives his Cross.

We see two hands in both. We also see two heads in both. In this Eleventh Station, Christ is depicted in the red of suffering and martyrdom. The whole painting is suffused with the pain and suffering brought about by the hammer and nail being driven into the hand of Christ. The hammer reminds me of the type of hammer that strikes the hours on a bell (like Big Ben), and this calls to mind the words of Christ: 'Father the hour has come. Glorify your Son that your Son may glorify You' (John 17:1).

'Glorify your Son': the glory of God is shown in the device of the blue flower-eye, and in the colours that make up the crown of thorns, red, blue gold and green. We have reflected earlier on the symbolism of these colours; the colours of the two natures of Christ, the colours of the eternal and divine and in the green the colour representing new life. 'Unless a grain of wheat falls to the earth and dies, it will remain just a single grain; but if it dies it will bring forth a rich harvest' (John 12:24).

Looking at the two people depicted, Christ and the executioner, even though the whole painting is raw with pain, the face of Christ is at peace -'Father, into your hands I commend my spirit'.

Whereas the second person is showing strong emotions such as hatred, blood lust, anger - look at the mouth with teeth bared.

Look also at the eye, it's black; no flower symbol here. There is no life in this person's eye. At this moment we cannot see the 'image and likeness' of God. For all the emotion, this man is dead.

Again, as in the Second Station, the narrative of this painting is turned on its head. Christ is at peace, the executioner is in torment. The executioner cannot take Christ's life, and only Christ can give the executioner back his life. 'You refuse to come to me to have life' (John 5:40), 'I came that they may have life and have it more abundantly' (John 10:10).

I love you Jesus, my love above all things. I repent with my whole heart of having offended thee. Never permit me to separate myself from thee again, and grant that I may love thee always and then do with me what thy wilt.

Holy Mother, pierce me through;
in my heart each wound renew
of my Saviour crucified.

Death, where is your victory?

Twelfth Station
Jesus dies on the Cross

This is the Station that I have had most difficulty trying to understand. I struggle to get past the 'green' man' in the background: what am I looking at? I'm not sure how to interpret this part of the painting.

Norman Adams explained how he painted the Twelfth: At the time he was working on it, there were reports in the newspapers about a death row convict in America being put to death in the electric chair, and this influenced his design. In this twelfth Station, Adams saw the crown of thorns as shards bleached white in the electric shock of death. So I wondered if the green figure behind the cross was a prison officer at the execution? Or is it simply one of the Roman soldiers on Calvary? But neither of these ideas felt right.

Another thought I had was: could this be a representation of Death, Death that holds Christ for three days in the grave until the great moment of resurrection? Is this image a way of painting the great acclamation of faith from St Paul in his letter to the church in Corinth, 'Death where is your victory; death where is your sting?' (I Cor 15:55).

Norman Adams also spoke about the mental torture that a death row prisoner underwent, and I now think this is the key to interpretation. The 'green man' is a representation of the mental stress and anguish that people face at times in their lives. Those despairing eyes that stare out over Christ's head contrast with the peaceful repose that can be found in the face of the dead Christ; red from the pain of his passion but Christ's face is the still and peaceful visage of the 'beloved Son'.

Is the 'green man' hidden behind the cross? Or is he becoming one with it? Is the Cross, God's instrument of grace, drawing a response from the 'green man' just as the Crucifixion drew a response from the centurion: 'in truth this man was Son of God' (Mark 15:39).

Don't let the 'green man' frighten the life out of you: look on Christ who is 'the Way, the Truth and the Life' (John 14:5), and who said 'I have come that they may have life and have it more abundantly' (John 10:10).

I love you Jesus, my love above all things. I repent with my whole heart of having offended thee. Never permit me to separate myself from thee again, and grant that I may love thee always and then do with me what thy wilt.

Let met share with thee his pain,
who for all my sins was slain,
who for me in torments died.

O thou mother, font of love.

Thirteenth Station
Jesus is taken down from the Cross and placed in the arms of His Blessed Mother

This painting depicts the mystery of love.

The colours are gentle tints of the primary colours yellow, blue and red and, after the strong emotional red colours leading up to Christ's death on the Cross, are clearly a change of mood.

We see here Our Lady in the top half of the painting holding her Son in the bottom half. Let us enter into this Station through the figure of Our Lady.

The delicate colours call to mind the reference in the Book of Revelation to the Woman 'clothed with the sun and a crown of twelve stars around her head' (Revelation 12). This is the Woman 'full of grace' who consented to be the Mother of God, the Madonna; who gave birth in Bethlehem and laid her son 'wrapped in swaddling clothes' in a manger. (Am I reading too much into this or can I see a swaddled baby shape in her face?)

The Madonna is now the *Pietà*, taking the body of her beloved Son into her arms, and we see the tears of love and her hand tenderly cradling her Son: holding him close in death, just as she always had in life – 'Do whatever he tells you'. This is a most intimate moment in the story and mother and son are painted by Norman Adams as interlocking faces, becoming one.

Now moving down the painting, we look at the Son. Jesus, son of Mary, held in his mother's loving hands is also the beloved Son of the Father. The presence of God the Father is often symbolised in Christian art with a 'hand', reaching down from heaven in blessing. So is it fanciful to see the hand here as being both that of Our Lady and the symbolic hand of the Father who is one with the Beloved Son: The mystery of love, both human and divine?

All the Stations painted by Norman Adams are the same dimensions, except for this station which is smaller than the others. This device helps us to understand that this is an intimate Holy Family moment in which we are privileged to share.

I love you Jesus, my love above all things. I repent with my whole heart of having offended thee. Never permit me to separate myself from thee again, and grant that I may love thee always and then do with me what thy wilt.

Let me mingle tears with thee,
mourning Him Who mourned for me,
all the days that I may live.

You who lift me up from the gates of death

Fourteenth Station
Jesus is buried in the tomb

For me, this painting is like looking into an overgrown garden through a wrought iron gate.

The Garden image: If we read St John's account of the burial of Christ we are told that Jesus was buried in a garden with a new tomb in it: 'At the place where he had been crucified there was a garden, and in this garden a new tomb in which no one had yet been buried. Since it was the Jewish Day of Preparation and the tomb was nearby, they laid Jesus there' (Jn19:41). We also read in St John's gospel that Mary of Magdala, when she first met the risen Christ, 'supposing him to be the gardener' asked where Christ has been put.

Gardens are full of flowers and Norman Adams has used the motif of flowers throughout his Stations of the Cross to express the spiritual relationships between the persons found on the Way of the Cross. Now, in this final bouquet Adams brings them all together.

The strongest colour we see in the garden is purple, colour of mourning: we are burying a loved one. Purple is also the 'royal' colour; and the loved one we are burying is a king.

At the bottom of the painting we see a strong, dark root system forming a barrier: the gulf between the living and the dead. But from these roots we can see stems and shoots sprouting up through the picture, producing all kinds of flowers. From the root of death appears the shoot of new life. Unless a grain of wheat falls to the ground and dies it remains a single grain: but if it dies it produces a rich harvest, some thirty, some sixty, some a hundredfold.

Remember who it is that we have buried: Jesus Christ, the Messiah, whom the prophet Isaiah described as the 'rod of Jesse..., he who rises up to rule the nations, and in him the nations will put their hope' (Isaiah 11:10). So even as we bury Christ we know this is not the end; he will rise again. Adams paints this hope of resurrection for us in the pink tones at the top of the painting. Together with the purples, the pink hues are the most dominant parts of the painting.

The image of the garden also reminds us of the Story of Creation and God walking in the Garden of Eden with Adam. This leads us on to the Fall and our need of redemption: to be re-created through the eighth day of Resurrection. 'Be gracious to me, Lord, you who lift me up from the gates of death' (Ps 9:13).

The gate image: Jesus is recorded in the Gospels as calling himself the Good Shepherd and described himself as the gate or door to the sheepfold. We need to go through this 'gate' to reach our 'hope'. Through the gate is the only way: Christ is the Way to Eternal Life.

In the painting, this garden gate is made from stems and branches: Jesus is the vine and we are the branches. If we remain in him we will grow. Read chapter 15 of St John's Gospel as a meditation on this station.

In popular culture we speak of 'the pearly gates' of heaven. The origin of this saying is in the Book of Revelation where St John describes his vision of the new Jerusalem as having gates made from pearls (Rev 21:21). In our painting the pearl pink is the dawn of a new day: it is resurrection and heaven. And we see the lozenge shapes reflecting the Divinity and the glory of the saints. A good place to end our Stations. But they are not quite finished.

Look again at the top left hand corner where we see a thin band of blue colour. Remember the symbolism of blue and how we interpreted it in the Fourth Station? (Our Lady, body and soul in heaven.)

Here the blue is reminding us that because of the great events told in the Stations, we too can hope for Heaven. It is also reminding us that Christ told us he would 'come again' on the Last Day: and after that those who were one with him would once again be united body and soul in eternal praise of the Father.

Now the story is told: now it is finished! The last words of Christ on the Cross: '*consummatum est*'.

'When a farmer prepares to till the soil he must put on clothing and use tools that are suitable. So Christ, our heavenly king, came to till the soil of mankind devastated by sin. He assumed a body and, using the cross as his ploughshare, cultivated the barren soul of man... And when he had ploughed the soul with the wood of the cross, he planted in it a most lovely garden of the Spirit, that could produce for its Lord and God the sweetest and most pleasant fruit of every kind' (From a Homily attributed to St Macarius, 28).

I love you Jesus my love above all things:
I repent with my whole heart
for having offended you.
Never permit me to separate myself
from you again.
Grant that I may love you always,
and then do with me what you will.